Inland Waters

by Elizabeth Ring · Photographs by Dwight Kuhn

BLACKBIRCH PRESS

An imprint of Thomson Gale, a part of The Thomson Corporation

THOMSON
™
GALE

Detroit • New York • San Francisco • San Diego • New Haven, Conn. • Waterville, Maine • London • Munich

For more information, contact
Blackbirch Press
27500 Drake Rd.
Farmington Hills, MI 48331-3535
Or you can visit our Internet site at http://www.gale.com

Photo Credits: Cover, all photos © Dwight Kuhn Photography

LIBRARY OF CONGRESS CATALOGING-IN-PUBLICATION DATA

Ring, Elizabeth, 1920-
  Inland waters / by Elizabeth Ring; Photographs by Dwight Kuhn
    p. cm. — (Communities in nature)
  Includes bibliographical references and index.
  ISBN 1-4103-0317-9 (lib. : alk. paper)
  1. Freshwater organisms—Juvenile literature. I. Title II. Series: Ring, Elizabeth, 1920–. Communities in nature.
  QH96.16.R56 2005
  578.76—dc22
                                                    2004016229

Printed in the United States of America
10 9 8 7 6 5 4 3 2 1

Introduction

Beside rivers and streams, you watch freshwaters tumble and weave over rocks, logs, and strong, waving reeds. Beside lakes and ponds, you look into still waters that mirror the sky's changing light. A trout fish streaks through a stream. A tadpole wriggles around in a pond. A coyote wets its dry tongue at the water's edge. Wherever you look, you find wild creatures living out their short or long lives—wherever the waters stay fresh and clean.

A thirsty coyote drinks cool, fresh water at the water's edge.

3

At the
Pond

Every April, my pond wakes up. It has been sleeping the winter away—beneath the ice I skate on top of when the pond freezes over. Springtime warms up the pond. Water lilies send up their flat leaves that look like floating green plates. Then, one by one, fat lily flowers bloom. Spring peepers send out their creaky frog songs. Under the lily pads, all kinds of pond creatures squirm into new life.

Water lily pads and blossoms float on the calm surface of a woodland pond.

By June, everything in the pond is going full steam. One day, I caught a tadpole in my net. It was about to turn into a frog—ready to hop out of the pond. All spring, hundreds of tadpoles swim and change shape in the pond. At first, when they hatch from their eggs, tadpoles don't have feet or tails. They breathe through gills, the way fish do, and they grow tails that look just like a fish's tail.

A pond is full of creatures to catch in a net—to get a close look.

A tadpole will swim underwater until it loses its tail and hops onto the land.

After a few weeks, tadpoles grow legs and start losing their tails. Grown frogs have no tail at all and they breathe through lungs, the way land animals do. The tadpole I caught will grow up to live in the woods. But, next spring, it will come back to the pond to mate and start a new frog family.

Newts look something like snaky, red-spotted tadpoles with tiny legs. Like tadpoles, they are land animals that start out their lives in the pond. They breathe through gills at first, too. When they crawl out onto land, juvenile newts (called "red efts") live in damp woods. After two to seven years, newts mature and go back to the water to live out their lives and breed.

You can always find dragonflies zinging around over the pond. Dragonflies spend most of their lives underwater as nymphs. Nymphs have little heads, big eyes, and no wings. They are young dragonflies—just as caterpillars are young moths or butterflies. One time, I watched an adult dragonfly creeping out of its nymph skin. Its new wings were so filmy and thin, I wondered if it could possibly fly. It did!

Opposite page: Newts are small salamanders that live both underwater and in damp woods. Right: Emerging at night, this dragonfly leaves behind the skin it wore as a nymph in the pond.

9

Painted turtles sun themselves in the pond. To warm up their cold-blooded bodies they crawl on top of plants, rocks—and even on top of each other. When they're warm, they stumble around like toy armored tanks. Or they swim, flapping their short, webbed feet, as if they're waving wide, stubby fans. Painted turtles have mostly dark green top shells with yellow shells under their bellies. Some look as if they've been painted with little red spots.

Two painted turtles lift out of the pond to warm themselves in the sun.

Mallard ducks live on the pond all summer long. The male duck is the flashy one, with his shiny green head, yellow beak, and a white necklace around his throat. He lands on the water, shakes his wings, and checks out the pond. Then, he sails away, looking proud of himself. He doesn't exactly look proud when he feeds, though. He dips his whole head in the water and lifts his tail end in the air. Then, he looks more like a clown.

A mallard duck lands on the pond and shakes water from its wet wings.

An egret stalks the pond's edge, searching for fish, frogs, or snakes to stab with its beak.

An egret always looks proud. It could be a statue, standing so still at the edge of the pond. When it steps through the water, stalking its prey, it lifts it long black legs daintily. You would never catch it sticking its rear in the air. It doesn't duck for its food. It simply aims its beak and stabs a fish, frog, or snake, hardly wetting its head.

Shy pumpkinseed sunfish hide among the pond's weeds.

You can usually find schools of "punkies" trying to hide near the edge of the pond. The egret is probably looking for them in the weeds. These bright-colored fish are called pumpkinseed sunfish. And they're shaped something like flat pumpkin seeds. They open their little mouths wide as they feed on insects, ants, beetles, fish eggs, and worms. Sometimes they nibble on the plants they hide beneath.

I see redwing blackbirds out over the pond. They often perch on cattail stalks that are brown in the summer, white in the fall. The tall, thick bunches of cattails are one of their favorite places to nest. You can't see the male blackbird's red wings very well, except when he spreads them wide open to fly. In the spring and fall, you can hear the male redwings calling all day— *konk-ka-reeee* or *oak-a-leee*. It sounds to me as if they're saying: "Look at meee! Look at meeeeee!"

On a fall day, a redwing blackbird perches on a frazzled cattail stalk.

One of the reasons I don't wade barefoot in the pond is that giant water bugs live there—and they bite. They're big, brown bugs, as long as my thumb. They have sharp beaks and fat, claw-like front legs, and they zoom around, attacking frogs and fish. As fierce as they are, I once saw a male water bug carefully carrying rows of eggs on his back. The male will care for the eggs for about three weeks—until the eggs hatch.

A fierce, biting water bug gently carries its eggs on its back.

Green frogs don't dart around and attack their prey the way water bugs do. They just wait at the edge of the pond for an insect, spider, tadpole, or small snake to come by. In the spring, each male frog sings his mating songs. His flat, twangy voice sounds like a loose violin string. You can tell a male frog by his round ears, twice as big as his bulgy eyes. The female's ears are small. Green frogs live close to water when they're fully grown. They don't take to the woods.

Green frogs haunt the pond, looking for insects and singing their spring mating songs.

I wish I could watch my tadpole grow into a frog, but it belongs in the water until it is old enough to live on the land. Well, I'll see lots of frogs all summer long. Maybe one of them will be the one I put back in the pond. I'll never know. They all look a lot alike.

Catching a tadpole in your net lets you examine it for a bit before letting it go.

By the
Stream

By the stream, where the water never stands still, foamy ripples roar over waterfalls and whisper around bends. The stream never looks quite the same from one day to the next. It runs high when it rains and sinks low in dry weather. It wears its banks down and builds sand piles on its bed. Fast or slow, the water always runs cool.

Cool, fresh water crashes over rocks in a rushing stream.

We kneel down on the rocks to get close to the stream. We see bunches of things we've seen before—frogs and fishes and snakes. But each time we visit the nature park—where the stream runs—we find something new. The park naturalists are there to tell us about what we're looking at.

You find all kinds of creatures in the stream—especially if get down on your knees to see.

The last time we were here, we saw some young blackflies. They were in what's called their larval state. The larvae looked like black worms, wiggling in the water near the stream's edge. The stream runs fast in that spot, but the larvae have hooks on their tail ends. The hooks hold them to rocks. Brushes around their mouths catch pieces of algae and other food bits and sweep them into their mouths. You can get close to larvae but not to adults. Adult blackflies grow wings. They fly all around you, and they bite very hard.

Blackfly larvae swarm in the stream before they grow up, grow wings—and bite.

Caddisfly nymphs keep themselves safe by covering their bodies with stones and twigs.

We saw a young caddisfly in the water one day. This insect is called a nymph before it grows up and gets wings. You can hardly see the nymph's white, wormy body at all. The nymph has glued stones and twigs all over itself. The case protects it from fish and birds. An adult caddisfly looks like a moth. We wouldn't mind meeting one of them. Caddisflies don't bite at all. They just fly.

Another day, we were lucky enough to see a mayfly just as it crawled out of its nymph skin. Mayflies spend about two years in the water, as nymphs. As adults, they fly for one or two days, mate, and die. Then, the female mayflies drop hundreds of eggs over the stream. The eggs sink and, later, hatch into new nymphs—and start the cycle all over again.

A mayfly crawls out of its nymph skin, ready to spread its new wings and fly off.

Dainty water striders speed on top of the water without ever sinking in.

Speedy water striders are the most fun to watch. You have to wonder how they can dart around on the water like that, looking for small insects to eat! They use their six crooked legs like paddles—the way you use oars to row a boat. Their feet make little dents in the water, but the bugs never sink in. We found out that they float because striders don't weigh very much. And they have little hairs on their body and legs and a waxy coat on their feet. They're as waterproofed as an insect can be.

You see salamanders in the water or out on the bank of the stream. They looked like little lizards, to us. But, the naturalist told us, the "sallies" are really related to frogs and toads. They eat insects and worms. They have very long tails that they can drop off if they're caught by a snake or a bird. Two lines down a salamander's back tell you it's a—guess what—a two-lined salamander. That's its name.

A two-lined salamander wriggles like a snake on the streambed.

You can tell a three-spined stickleback fish by its name, too. You just count the spines sticking up on its back. There are nine-spined sticklebacks, as well. All sticklebacks are little, minnow-sized fish. During mating season, male sticklebacks build a nest of small plants. Females swim through a tunnel into the nest and lay eggs. The males fertilize the eggs. And then, when young fish hatch, the males take care of them for a few weeks—until they're ready to take care of themselves.

A three-legged stickleback fish uses small plants to build a nest by a streambed.

Brook trout are like other trout in the stream, except they have dark, wavy marks on their backs, not black spots like other trout fish. Young trout eat insects and other soft food. Later, they also eat crayfish, snails, frogs, and other fish. When trout have gotten to be good-sized adults, lots of people like to go fishing for them. The frisky trout always put up a good fight before they get reeled in.

Frisky brook trout, known by the wavy lines on their backs, live and play among the stream's rocks.

Kingfishers really know how to fish. The big, pigeon-sized bird will sit—sometimes for hours—on a tree branch and stare at the stream. Then it dives into the water and catches a salamander or crayfish. When it spears a fish with its long beak, it carries it to his perch. It tosses the fish up in the air and catches it again—the way you'd toss popcorn into your mouth. This kingfisher is called "belted" because of the gray belt on its white throat.

A kingfisher dives into the stream to spear a fish with its long beak.

33

The water shrew is some hunter, too. It often goes after worms and fly nymphs. A shrew can swim, dive, and even run on the bottom of the stream. One time, we saw a shrew run a short way on top of the water—without falling in. We found out it could do that because hairs on the shrew's big back feet trap bubbles of air. The bubbles act something like air-filled pontoons that keep boats afloat. They don't let the shrew sink. But a shrew wouldn't do that all the time—the way water striders do.

This water shrew dives, swims, and runs on the streambed, hunting for fly nymphs and worms to eat.

Lots of land animals come to the stream from fields and woods. We watched a white-tailed deer one warm, windy day. It was a female, a doe. Her big eyes looked this way and that. Her big radar ears twitched. She slowly tore some leaves off a plant. She didn't see or hear us, squatted down in the bushes on the other side of the stream. We guessed it was because the wind was blowing our scent away from her. Finally, when she thought no danger was near, she stepped into the stream for a drink.

This white-tailed deer checks out its surroundings before taking a drink from the stream.

Crayfish are fierce predators, and hunt for small creatures to catch in their claws.

We wondered if the deer's nose would get nipped by one of those crayfish that live in the stream. The crayfish's claws pinch hard. They're as strong as a crab's claws—and crayfish are fierce. They attack snails, worms, tadpoles, fish eggs, and dead fish. A crayfish probably wouldn't go after a deer, though—we thought. That's the next thing we'll have to ask the naturalist about.

My friend caught a crayfish, one day, in a net. It looked like a small shrimp. When we examined the crayfish upside down, we could see all its parts. Behind its claws, it has four pairs of legs. It uses those legs to walk and to poke into cracks between rocks, looking for food. Then, right under its belly, are five pairs of swimmerets, little feathery legs that help crayfish swim. Females use their swimmerets to carry their eggs.

The crayfish didn't pinch us, and we put it back in the stream. It swam away backward, waving its tail. We waved back good-bye and went on up the stream—to see what else lives in this cool, freshwater world.

This crayfish waves its claws and legs at its captor—before it's put back in the stream.

More About Inland Waters

Belted kingfisher

Belted kingfishers build large, unlined nests in stream banks. Tunnels that lead to the nests are 4 to 15 feet (1.2 to 4.6m) long. Both parents tend their five to seven chicks.

Blackfly larvae (blackfly young) form cocoons, from which adult flies emerge. Adults are sometimes called "buffalo gnats," because their humped bodies are buffalo shaped.

Brook trout are related to salmon, whitefish, chars, and other kinds of trout fish. They live in lakes, rivers, and streams where waters are cool and clear. Their nests are also called redds.

Caddisflies look like moths and butterflies, but they are not related. After adult caddisflies mate, the females run on the surface of the water (not really flying) to drop their eggs.

Coyotes are members of the dog family—about the size of a collie. They live in forests, grasslands, high mountains, and low plains—wherever food and freshwater can be found.

Crayfish are crustaceans (animals with shells around their soft bodies). Crayfish are also known as crawdads, crawfish, and freshwater lobsters.

Coyote

Green frog

Dragonflies have six legs and four wings. They can fly 50 to 60 miles (80 to 97km) an hour. Their hairy legs are good for perching on branches—but not for walking.

Giant water bugs have compound (many-lensed) eyes. A tube at a water bug's rear end acts like a snorkel and brings air to spiracles (breathing holes) in its body.

Great white egrets are herons that nest in colonies called heronries. The birds build their stick nests anywhere between the ground and treetops. They can live up to 22 years.

Green frogs are greenish brown with black spots. Most males have a yellow throat. Females lay a thousand or more eggs that hatch within a week to become tadpoles.

Mallard ducks are called dabbling ducks because they duck their heads in the water to feed. After mating season, males (drakes) group together. Females raise from five to twelve ducklings.

Mayflies are sometimes called "dayflies" because of the adults' short lives of one or two days.

Northern two-lined salamanders are active from February to November. After hatching from eggs laid in water, the larvae (young) look like frog tadpoles and, like fish, breathe through gills.

Painted turtles, like all turtles, have two shells—a carapace on top of their soft bodies, and a plastron underneath. They live to be about ten years old in the wild.

Painted turtle

Ponds are bodies of freshwater, usually 6 or 7 feet (1.8 or 2.1m) deep. They are smaller and more shallow than lakes. Their water temperature is usually the same as the air temperature.

Pumpkinseed sunfish make round nests among plants in ponds. Females lay 1,500 to 3,000 eggs. Males fertilize the eggs and guard the nests until the eggs hatch in three to five days.

Red-spotted newts are small salamanders that live in ponds and forests. In their juvenile (eft) stage on land, their skin is poisonous, which saves them from most predators.

Redwing blackbirds live around marshes and ponds. They make their nests of mud, plant fibers, and grass. Each season, both males and females may take more than one mate.

Redwing blackbird

Sticklebacks are small fish 1 to 4 inches (2.5 to 10.2cm) long. They have teeth and eat larvae, worms, and the eggs and young of other fish. They are prey to larger fish and to birds.

Streams are natural bodies of fresh, running waters. They start at high headwaters and flow downhill. Brooks and creeks are small streams. Rivers are large streams that run to salt seas.

Water shrews are small animals that weigh ⅜ to ⅝ ounces (10.6g to 17.7g). They live along stream banks among roots and rocks. Trout, snakes, owls, and weasels are their main predators.

Water striders stride forward 100 times their own body length—in one second. Fossils (dead bodies) of water striders over 100 million years old have been found.

Water shrew

White-tailed deer

White-tailed deer often live close to forest streams. There they find water to drink, plants to eat, and trees to take cover in when predators threaten them.

Wood frog tadpoles feed on algae and leaves in ponds and streams. As adult frogs, they live in the woods and feed mostly on insects.

For More Information

Julie Becker, *Animals of the Ponds and Streams.* St. Paul, MN: EMC/Paradigm, 1977.

Jim Brandenberg, *The North American Prairie.* New York: Walker, 1995.

Karen Edelstein, *Pond and Stream Safari.* Ithaca, NY: Cornell University, 1993.

Paul Fleisher, *Pond.* Tarrytown, NY: Marshall Cavendish, 1999.

————, *Mountain Stream.* Tarrytown, NY: Marshall Cavendish, 1999.

Ann Morgan, *Field Book of Ponds and Streams.* New York: Putnam, 1930.

Missouri Botanical Garden (http://mbgnet.mobot.org). Ponds, lakes, rivers and streams.

U.S. Geological Survey, (http://ga.water.usgs.gov/edu/). The Earth's freshwater and salt waters.

Index